How to Make a Video on Y

Entrepreneur Series

M. Usman

Mendon Cottage Books

JD-Biz Publishing

Download Free Books!

http://MendonCottageBooks.com

[Entrepreneur Book Series](#)

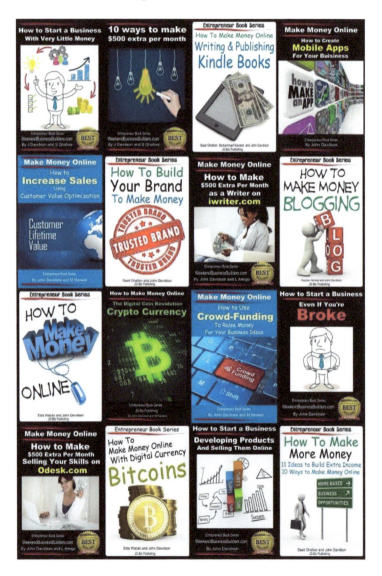

Table of Contents

Preface

It's normal to have doubts on whether your videos are worth showing to other people, let alone if you should upload them to YouTube. However, the truth is that there are no rules as to what makes a good video. If you enjoy watching it, then there is a good chance that others will also find it entertaining.

But, YouTube is not just there so you can upload videos to entertain people. You can also use it to promote your website, promote a certain product, educate people, etc.

Making it even better, the number of YouTube users has grown tremendously in recent years. For you, this is an opportunity to get your videos watched by a lot of people. Statistics show that YouTube gets 1 billion unique users every month.

In this book, you will learn the steps you need to follow when you want to make a YouTube video. I will give you tips on how you can have better pictures as well as sounds. If you will be doing some editing, the book also has tips on that.

You will also find info on promotion, making money with YouTube, lighting, and more.

So without wasting any more time, let's get started. Millions are eagerly waiting to see your video.

Chapter 1: Come up with an Idea

You do not go to YouTube without knowing what you intend to watch. There is always a purpose. It could be that you want to see some of the funniest dance moves ever invented. Or you could be there to watch some of your favorite music videos. YouTube also has many silly jokes to brighten your day.

So before you make your video, you must have a goal you would like to achieve when the video ends. Are you trying to entertain, inform, express, or persuade the viewer?

Once you have an idea, you should write it on paper. This will enable you to objectively evaluate if people will enjoy watching a video on this subject. If you find it is not what people would want, then you can tweak it. Your job is to ensure that the video fulfills someone's need.

Here are types of videos that people make:

Vlogs – These are also known as video blogs. Usually, they are a series of videos released regularly. The creator normally has a specific subject they talks about. If the topic is something people enjoy, they can build a decent list of subscribers.

Reviews – Remember the last time you wanted to buy something? You surely read some reviews of the product and spent some time watching its reviews on YouTube. These kinds of videos are very popular on this website.

Comedy – Then there are the silly videos that have made YouTube so popular. These are there for your entertainment. The creator has one thing in mind when producing these—make you laugh until you break your diaphragm. If you are creative, there is nothing stopping you from making videos like these.

Tutorials – Would you like to know how to bake a cake? Watching a video is easier than reading about how to do it. And, if you would like to solve a certain equation, watching how it's done, again, is way easier. So, if you know how to do something, you might as well make a video about it.

As you will be thinking about your idea, it also pays to know how long your video will be. The rule of thumb is that it must be fairly short. Anything longer than 15 minutes will not get a lot of views unless it's important. So, make sure that you only have what is necessary in the video.

Furthermore, you must make sure that you identify your audience before you make the video. Doing this will ensure that you:

- make videos that your audience will like

- use their language

- choose the best ways to promote your videos

Chapter 2: Tools You Need

To make a video, you at least need a camcorder. But for better results, you also need to invest in other tools. These can make the difference between an amateur video and a professional one.

Let's discuss the tools you need:

Camcorder
If this was 10 or 20 years ago, you would have to spend hundreds of dollars just to get a good camcorder. But thanks to advancements in technology, you can now make professional-looking videos without breaking the bank.

Phone
The easiest and probably cheapest way to record a video is to your use your camera phone. This is assuming that you have a phone with a decent

camera. So, no need to invest in anything else here.

Making it even better is that your phone goes where you go. So if you find a moment worthy of making a YouTube video of, you can always jump to the opportunity. And if you do not like the way your camera app works, you can download another one—there are lots of them.

However, a phone's camcorder is not suitable for long videos. Also, you may have trouble stabilizing the picture, resulting in a video that's shaky.

Webcam

If all you will be filming is yourself, your laptop's webcam is another good option. Just like with the phone, this is also a cheap option because almost all laptops now have this. However, you may sacrifice quality by going this route. And, you have limited angles to shoot from, as the camera is fixed to the laptop.

Dedicated camcorder

If you are serious about making videos that will wow your viewers, then get yourself a dedicated camcorder. Although these have also fallen in price, the best ones start from around $300. Apart from giving you impressive pictures, these may also have the option of connecting a standalone microphone.

Audio

Viewers can endure a terrible video, but if the sound is bad, they will walk away even if the video is great. This just shows how important it is to get the audio right. Although your phone, laptop, or camcorder has a mic, you may have to get another one for better results.

This will ensure that only the subject is the prominent voice in the video. Again, it will give you flexibility to position the mic where you know you will achieve better results.

Most camcorders have a mic in jack, so use it. Another option is to get a USB mic. And if you have the money, then you can invest in a mic and a preamp.

Storage
Storage is one thing you shouldn't compromise. And knowing that the price of storage has fallen considerably, you really have no excuse of not investing in this.

A Good Computer
If you will just be uploading your videos to YouTube without any post processing, then you do not need a super-powerful computer. Even a cheap Chromebook will do just fine.

But, if you will be editing your videos, a decent computer is crucial. This can be a Mac or a PC, as both get the job done. As for the processor, an i5 or i7 should do it.

However, all this is nothing without lots of ram. Ideally, you should have at least 4GB. But 8GB is recommended. If you can take it even higher, 16GB to be specific, then it's even better.

Also, you will need to have a fast hard drive with lots of space. A 1TB hard drive should be enough to get you going.

Headphones
Although these are not always necessary, they will make your work a lot easier. It is better to realize that the audio is wrong while shooting rather than when you are editing. So if you do not want to go through the hassle of shooting again, it pays to get a good pair of headphones.

Chapter 3: Introduction to Lighting

Light is your best friend if you want to make good videos. This is a secret all good videographers know. Although the camera lens is made to see the world in the same way you do, it does not.

So, you must spend time with it to see the world the way it sees it.

Here are some tips you must keep in mind:

Make your videos during the day – The sun is one of the most important ingredients you need to make good videos. So, you must make sure that you shoot your videos during the day. However, if you are shooting outside, it is best to not do it in the afternoon. This is the worst time to make a video. The sun is high in the sky, shining its brightest, thus washing out much of the color.

If you are inside, then you must make sure that you open all windows and doors, as this will let in enough light.

Shoot from different angles – Since you may be learning the ropes of using a camcorder, you may not know where to place the camera to get the best picture with your existing lighting conditions. So, I advise you to try shooting from different angles. When you move the camera, you will see that the light on the picture will also change.

Play with different settings – Your camera has a lot of settings that determine how it sees light. This is especially true with a camcorder, as phones and webcams have limited features. So if you find these settings, do not be afraid to play with them. Try changing a few things and see how they affect your picture.

Your camcorder's manual should have instructions on how you can tweak these settings. If doesn't, then you can do a quick search online.

Recording in Artificial Light

You will not always have the option of shooting your videos with light from the sun. In such situations, you will need to use artificial lights, and these can cost from around $1,000 and up.

Here are the types of lights you will need:

Key light – This is your main light, and it is used to illuminate the front of your subject. Usually, it is placed at a 45 degrees angle from the subject.

Fill light – This light fills the shadows caused by the key light. Without this, your image would look dramatic. You must, however, ensure that the fill light does not create a second shadow. If it does, you can dim it or move it away from the subject. The fill light is placed on the other side of the key light.

Backlight – As the name says, this is placed at the back of the subject, and above his head. Although some do not agree to the use of this light, it can add a nice effect to your image.

By placing your lights in this position, you will make what is known as 3-point lighting. If your video was looking flat and boring, lighting this way can spice it up.

Since setting up lights can take time, it's better that you dedicate some space for them. Then, when you feel like making a video, you will not be wasting time arranging things. Optionally, you can just mark the spots where these light go.

Chapter 4: Tips on Recording Your Voices

As stated previously, you can get away with a bad video. But, if you pair it with bad audio, it's all over for you. Although audio is an important part of video making, many tend to ignore it. They believe that if the picture is good, then they have met the minimum requirements of a good video.

However, this is wrong, and your viewers will penalize you for it. In this chapter, I will give you some useful tips for recording your audio.

Here they are:

Speak clearly – Regardless of the importance of the words in the video, you must make sure that they are as clear as possible. If you are not the one speaking, it will even be better as you will likely spot all the mistakes the subject is making.

If you are the one saying the words, but cannot manage to get them across clearly, it's better that you do some diction exercises. Also, standing up will help as it opens the airway and gives you a chance to fill your lungs fully.

To improve your overall speaking abilities, you must practice speaking. So try recording yourself on your phone.

Speak loudly – This is another thing that amateurs get wrong all the time. Mostly, it is the result of lacking confidence. So just breathe and speak as loudly as you can. Do not be afraid of making a mistake; you will have a chance to edit your video before uploading it to YouTube.

Talking loud does not mean that you should scream. You will alienate your viewers.

Mic must be close to the subject – If the mic is too far from the person speaking, you can guarantee that your viewers will not hear the words being spoken. And this will also force the subject to scream which will strain his/her vocal cords.

As if not enough, the mic can pick up a lot of background noise, thereby ruining your video.

To ensure that you have the flexibility of getting the mic closer to the subject and still bing able to place the camera where you want, buying a stand-alone mic is the way to go. This is why microphones built into the camcorder, phone, or webcam are not ideal.

Close windows and doors – If there is a lot of noise outside, it's best that you close all windows and doors. However, by doing this, I assume that you have artificial lights.

Record when people are in bed – If there is still a lot of noise after you have closed all windows and doors, your best option is to record when people are in bed.

Note that you do not always need to record your audio the same time you make the video. If you want, you can add the audio later. This is used in cartoons as well as some movies. The fact that you are not concerned with audio as you make the video gives you a chance to concentrate on getting the best picture.

Chapter 5: Tips to Enhance Your Video

Sometimes, beauty lies in the smallest details. Although some of the tips I am about to give below may seem insignificant, they pack a punch that may well spur your video to greatness. Even better, some of these tips are very easy to apply.

Have a tripod – If you want to have a video that looks like you mean business, you better put your camera on a stable surface. And simply, that surface is a tripod. Although these can be really cheap, I would advise that you save some money and buy the best you can afford.

Not only do cheap tripods break easily, but they also dance to the wind, which defeats the purpose of buying one in the first place. So even though it may look as if you are saving money in the beginning, the cost of buying replacements will quickly add up.

Stay away from digital zoom - If you have this on your camera, and I bet you do, simply stay away from it. Not only does it add pixels to you video, it also leaves your viewers dizzy if you use it a lot. And, this puts a thought in your viewer's head that reads, "This is nothing more than amateur work."

If you have optical zoom, that's a lot better. But still, you should not use it as if your life depends on it.

If you want the subject to fill the frame, get closer to them. And talking about getting closer to your subject, you must…

Use wide shots sparingly – Although you may want to capture everything that is happening around, you must keep these kinds of shots to a minimum. They are great if you want to introduce the scene and add variety to your video—now and then. Because, if you use them excessively, your viewers will lose focus of what's going on.

What you ultimately want are close ups. These focus on the subject and nothing else.

Shoot from different angles – YouTube viewers have a lot to see, as videos are added every minute, so you must ensure that your video is not boring. A good way to avoid that is to ensure that you keep changing the angles from which you show your subject. Otherwise, your viewers will be bored and will leave. As they say, variety is the spice of life, so use it to your advantage.

Pay attention to the background – A background is there to just support your video. It should not, in any way, become the main center of focus, or it will distract the viewer from watching your video.

Have enough storage – This was said earlier, but it deserves another mention. If you will be making your videos away from home, you do not want to stop filming just because you have run out of storage. So, before you leave home, ensure that you have lots of this.

This will give you a chance to take as many shots as you can. Also, they will be of higher quality.

Have spare batteries – Just like with storage, there is nothing more irritating than watching your battery die. So before you close your bag, make sure that your camera is properly charged. Additionally, ensure that you have taken spare batteries.

Chapter 6: Introduction to Editing

It is not always necessary to edit your video, but then, that means you should know when to press the pause button, which can be a lot of work. I have seen some really good videos on YouTube without any editing.

If you want to add a touch of professionalism, however, it's vital that you edit your work. You can, for example, add effects, hide some of the mistakes you made, etc.

But before you can think of editing, you will need to have two things:

A computer – Although you can also edit on your phone, the best results are likely to be achieved on a computer. Editing softwares are resource hungry, so this is where a computer with impressive specs comes in handy.

For more on what kind of a computer you need for video editing, take a look at chapter two.

Software – You will also need to have software to edit your videos. Here are some of the most popular ones:

- Movie Maker – This is available for windows and it's free

- iMovie - This is for mac and the computer version is also free

- Light Works - If you do not mind the steep learning curve, this is a good option, as it comes with lots of powerful features

- Final Cut Pro – This is one of the best softwares your money can buy. It has just about everything you need

- Adobe Premiere Effects - Another good option for those with the money

If you have these tools, you have almost everything you need to get started. Here are some more ideas to keep in mind:

Take multiple shots – If you do not take multiple shots of your video, your editing abilities will be limited. Therefore, I encourage you to shoot as many shots as possible. And knowing that it is difficult to get everything right in one shot, this is very important advice.

Shots should not be too long or too short – If your shots are short, you will annoy your viewers. However, if they are too long, you will bore them. So make sure that you have a balance between the two. Ideally, the minimum must be 2 seconds and the maximum can be 10 seconds. However, these rules are not set in stone. Feel free to break them as you see fit.

Add effects necessarily – If you will be adding effects, make sure that they are necessary. Doing it just for the sake of it is not the best way to edit a video. While you may think the effects will give your video a wow factor, your viewers will find them distracting. Besides, they are not there to watch you show off how good you are with the effects.

Add an intro and ending – Having a nice opening to your video puts the viewer at ease. It makes them realize that you take your work seriously and that they will not waste their time watching your video. Since you have an opening, you must also have an ending.

There are no rules as to what you can include in the intro or ending. But many have theme music, the name of their channel, and a call to action at the end.

Chapter 7: Uploading a Video to YouTube

Now that you have finished editing your video, it's time to upload it to YouTube. By getting to this part, I assume that you are happy with your video and are confident that viewers will like it.

The steps below will show you how to upload the video to YouTube using a computer. If your phone has an option of uploading to YouTube, you may also use that. Again, some video editing software also have this ability. But this chapter cannot cover everything, so we will just focus on uploading from a computer using a browser.

Here are the steps to follow:

1. Open your browser and type "www.youtube.com" in the URL bar.

2. Sign into your account. You will use your Google account to do this. If you do not have one, you can create it easily.

3. When logged in, click the "Upload" button. You will find this on the upper right-hand corner of the page.

4. Choose privacy – You will need to choose among "public," "private," and "enlisted." Public means the video can be seen by anyone. Private is where only you and those you select will have access to the video. As for enlisted, only those who have the link can watch the video.

5. Select the video you want to upload by clicking the big red button in the middle. A file browser will open and you will need to navigate to the location of your video. Alternatively, you can just drop your video it in this space.

6. The video will start uploading and you will see its progress.

7. You will have to add some details about your video. This includes a title, a description, and tags. You will learn more about this in the next chapter.

8. When the video is done uploading, YouTube will generate thumbnails for you. This is what people will see before they watch your video. So if you do not like what YouTube has selected for you, you can create your own thumbnails. Just make sure that they look professional and sell the video.

9. You will also need to select if you want to share the video with your friends. If you have a large social media presence, this is a good way to promote your video.

As you can see, the process of uploading a video to YouTube is not difficult.

If you are uploading the video from your phone or from video editing software, the process is not really different from the steps outlined above.

Chapter 8: Promoting Your Video

With lots of videos on YouTube, getting exposure is not easy. If you are not careful, your video will join the big list of other good videos that no one watches. So, you will need to be smart and promote your video appropriately.

Here are some tips you can use:

Title, description, and tags are important – If you are tired and feeling too lazy to come up with a good name for your video, then I would recommend that you wait until you are thinking straight. The title is what will get your viewer's attention, so it must be catchy. Additionally, it must have keywords, as search engines will need these to rank your video.

You must also ensure that you have properly written the description. Some viewers, as well as search engines, find this useful.

Use social media – If you have a large social media presence, then you can use it to promote your video. The most popular social networking sites are Facebook, Twitter, and Google+. But, there are others you may also find useful. You should ensure that you have an account on at least one of these.

Ask People to share, like, and comment – Even though this may seem like a desperate attempt to make your video popular, the truth is that it works. Getting a lot of views, likes, and shares will prove to others that the video is great. So, anyone seeing it will be tempted to know what the buzz is all about.

Ask bloggers to share your video – People with blogs are always on the lookout for new and interesting content. Therefore, if you know a certain blogger who may be interested in your video, it is always a good idea to reach out to them and ask if they can share it with their audience. If the video will be useful to their readers, they will likely agree to your request.

Encourage people to subscribe to your channel – If you can get a lot of people to subscribe to your channel, you can bet that you will always have someone ready to watch your new videos. Your subscribers will get notifications whenever you upload a new video to your channel.

Make lots of videos – No one will be willing to subscribe to your channel if it only has one or two videos. To ensure that this does not happen, it is important that you upload a lot of videos to your account. And these must be great videos.

Make a blog post about the video – If you have a website with a considerable number of readers, then you can write a post that relates to the video, and then you can embed this video in the post.

Hire a YouTube marketer – Are you serious about making it on YouTube, but do not have the time to promote your videos? Then get a YouTube marketer. You can find one on sites like Freelancer, UpWork, PeoplePerHour, etc.

Chapter 9: Making Money with YouTube

Who doesn't like making money from their efforts? I bet it's not you. However, making a substantial amount of money with YouTube requires hard work. You will need to make a lot of great videos, and at the same time, promote them.

If you can manage to grow your subscribers, making money becomes easier. It's just the beginning that's a lot of work.

Here are a few ways of making money with YouTube:

Promote Your Products
If you have something that you sell, you can promote it on YouTube. This could be an eBook, software, a t-shirt, or anything else. However, make sure

that you keep the balance between giving your viewers what they want and selling your products. If you sell too much, you will surely drive them away.

Do Affiliate Marketing

For those who do not want to go through the hassle of making their own products, promoting other people's products is the way to go. For each referral that ends up buying the product, you earn a commission. This is what is called affiliate marketing.

Although the commission is usually small, 2-10% in most situations, it can add up if you have a lot of viewers.

What you will need to do is pick a few products and focus on them. You can do reviews on these products or teach people how to use them. At the end of your video, you should include your affiliate link. This is what people will use to buy the product.

Popular websites with affiliate programs are Amazon, Ebay, ShareASale, and CJ Affiliate.

Make Money with Ads

If you have videos that people just love, you can make money through ads. Every time a viewer clicks an ad, you will get some money. Unfortunately, you will need a lot of viewers to succeed with this. But if your videos are what people are looking for, and you promote them, you will realize that this is easy.

Find a Sponsor

You can also make money by getting yourself a sponsor. The growth of YouTube has made companies realize that sponsoring a YouTube channel with a lot of viewers is a cheap way to get to new customers.

However, you must be ready to approach some companies for this opportunity. And you must keep on making great videos, as that is what the sponsor will want. Although you will not be making much with this, a few hundred bucks every month is better than nothing.

Use YouTube to Get Traffic to Your Website

Due to the growth of YouTube users, this website is slowly becoming one of the most resourceful ways for websites to increase their traffic. So if you have a website, you can use YouTube as a source of traffic.

But this assumes that you have monetized the website. You may do this by selling products on it, having ads, or doing affiliate marketing. So when people go from YouTube to your website, you can bet that they will make you some money.

Conclusion

I am sure that this book has helped you discover how you can make a YouTube video.

An important point to remember is that you do not need an expensive camera to make the best video. If your lighting conditions are good, you can end up with a pretty decent video. You just need to be creative with how you use your camera.

Additionally, you must never ignore the importance of sound in your video. If viewers can't hear anything, they will not be patient to see how it ends. Also, you must not be afraid of making mistakes when shooting—that's what editing is for.

But the most important thing to remember is to have a great idea for your video. Everything else that comes will depend on this. So make sure that you give this step your undivided attention.

And once you are done making your video and it's on YouTube, you must wear the hat of a marketer and start promoting it. If you do not do this, no one will find it, so it will get buried under other great videos that get no views. All your efforts and sweat will be in vain.

Good luck and I look forward to seeing your videos on YouTube!

References

https://pixabay.com/en/you-tube-icon-play-button-logo-red-897421/

https://pixabay.com/en/adult-cute-face-female-girl-15814/

https://pixabay.com/en/camera-photography-lens-equipment-690163/

https://pixabay.com/en/greenbox-director-instruction-very-964781/

https://pixabay.com/en/microphone-voice-over-music-759587/

https://pixabay.com/en/playmobil-photography-photographers-765110/

https://pixabay.com/en/technology-keyboard-computing-785742/

https://pixabay.com/en/hands-businesswoman-presentation-589476/

'https://pixabay.com/en/social-network-facebook-network-76532/

About the Author

Dr. Usman is an MD, now pursuing his post-graduation degree. As a medical doctor, he has deep insight in all aspects of health, fitness, and nutrition. He is a certified nutritionist and a personal trainer. With these qualifications, he has helped countless people reach their health, fitness, and weight loss goals.

Dr. Usman is an avid researcher with 20+ publications in internationally accepted peer reviewed journals. He is an accomplished writer with more than 5 years of writing experience. In this time, he has produced countless blogs, articles, and research work on topics related to health, fitness, and nutrition.

He is a published author with more than 100+ books published and several more in the pipeline.

Finally, he runs his own blog and posts health, fitness, and nutrition related articles there regularly. You can visit his blog at http://hcures.com/

Check out some of the other JD-Biz Publishing books

Gardening Series on Amazon

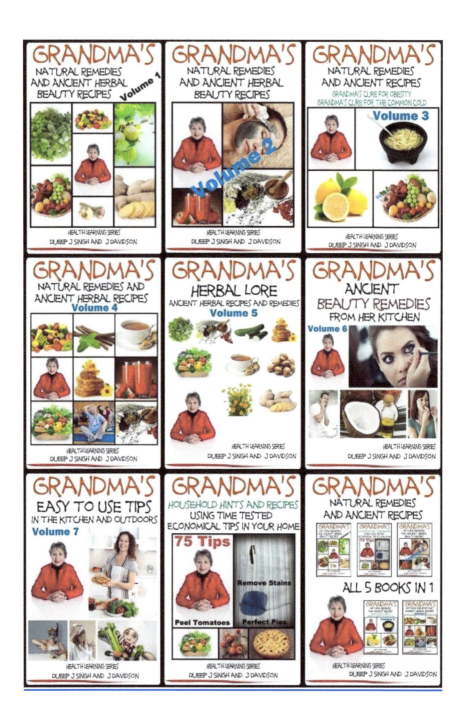

Country Life Books

Health Learning Series

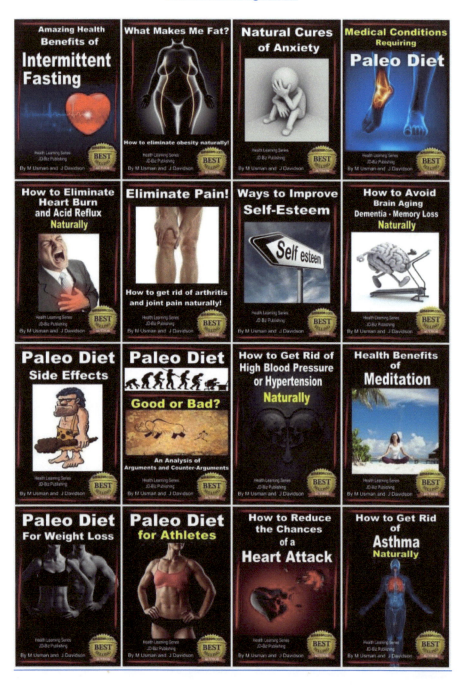

Amazing Animal Book Series

Learn To Draw Series

Entrepreneur Book Series

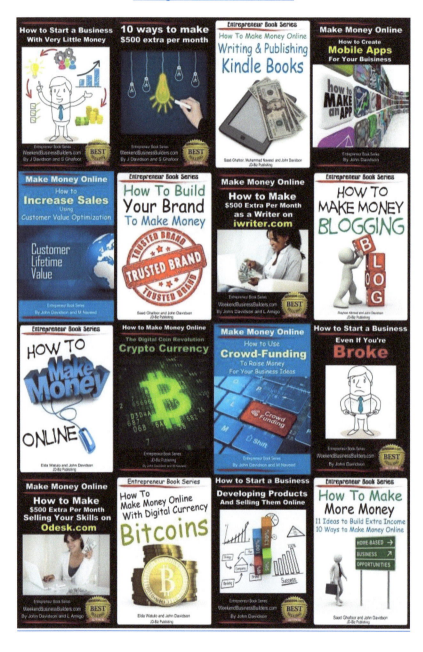

Our books are available at

1. Amazon.com

2. Barnes and Noble

3. Itunes

4. Kobo

5. Smashwords

6. Google Play Books

Download Free Books!
http://MendonCottageBooks.com

Publisher

JD-Biz Corp

P O Box 374

Mendon, Utah 84325

http://www.jd-biz.com/

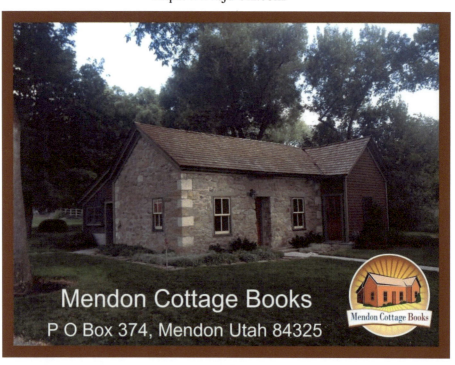

www.ingramcontent.com/pod-product-compliance
Lightning Source LLC
Chambersburg PA
CBHW041146050326
40689CB00001B/512